BERNADETTE
HER STORY

FRANÇOISE BOUCHARD

BERNADETTE
HER STORY
(1844-1879)

Translation by
Emma Cypher-Dournes

SALVATOR
103, rue Notre-Dame-des-Champs
F-75006 Paris

To my daughter and son-in-law
Marie-Hélène and Pierre Garnaud

Cover design by Isabelle de Senilhes
© Cover illustration: Sanctuaires Notre-Dame de Lourdes / EURL Basilic
of the Rosary

Interior layout by Arlant'Communication

© **Éditions Salvator**, Paris, 2007
103, rue Notre-Dame-des-Champs
F-75006 Paris
www.editions-salvator.com
contact@editions-salvator.com

ISBN 978-2-7067-0497-0

Foreword

A spring at the foot of the rock

Whether as a lone pilgrim or as part of a group, who has not felt intense emotion in front of the Massabielle Grotto? Who, when praying at the foot of the white marble statue, has not felt the presence, still strong today, of the Immaculate Conception? Who, when making their requests, has not been convinced that her Mother's heart has heard them?

Yet, without Bernadette Soubirous, we would not have Lourdes. She freed up this spring at the foot of the rock for us. She invites us to put aside everything that keeps us from finding the Source that brings Life and urges us to walk towards the "other world" where true Light shines.

In these pages let us discover the highlights of her "life of simplicity" and follow in her footsteps on the road leading to Jesus through Mary.

Chapter I

Like a single heart

The first fruit of love

Bernadette was born on Sunday January 7th 1844 at Lourdes. Her father, François Soubirous, worked as a miller at the Boly watermill. He earned a reasonable living, assisted by his wife, Louise Castérot.

François was 37 and Louise 18, but despite this difference in age they had married for love, a rare privilege at that time.

The birth of their first child, one year after their wedding, brought great delight to both parents. They named the baby girl Marie-Bernarde, and more intimately, Bernadette.

The empty cradle

Bernadette was barely ten months old when her mother fell ill[1]. Louise was pregnant again and had to stop breastfeeding her baby[2]. The child was reluctantly

---

1. See my book: *Sainte Bernadette, La Voie de la simplicité,* Éd. Salvator, Paris, 2006.
2. At that time, infants were not weaned before the age of two.

the care of Marie Laguës, a wet nurse living in
...s, a small village four kilometres from Lourdes.
Bernadette had just turned two when her parents were
finally able to take her back. Her return relieved some of
the sadness they had experienced after the death of their
second child just two months after being born. The whole
Castérot family shared in this joyful homecoming, particularly Bernarde, her godmother, who liked to say: "She
knows me as well as her mother!" A few months later,
Marie-Antoinette, known as Toinette, was born, followed
by Jean-Marie in 1851, adding to the joy of the family.

A predictable decline

Little by little the situation deteriorated at the watermill. There were a number of reasons: François and
Louise were illiterate and did not keep accounts. They
forgot to call in their dues from their customers and often
told them: "Pay us when you can!" So money was not
coming in. In addition, Louise always provided food to
the women who were waiting for the grain they had
brought to be milled; often the cost of feeding them was
higher than the money earned from milling their grain.

Furthermore, the millstones were worn-out. While
dressing the millstones to make them less smooth,
François was wounded in the eye by a fragment of stone
which would handicap him for the rest of his life. The
sieves were damaged. As he could not replace them,
François was reduced to producing flour of inferior
quality.

Moreover, industrial flourmills were taking a hold in the region and traditional mills could not compete with them. The combination of these factors meant that the Soubirous were heading for ruin.

United in effort

In 1854, they left the mill. Bernadette was ten and had been suffering from severe asthma for some time. François worked on a day-to-day basis, mainly at the Maisongrosse bakery and at Cazenave's carriage company (driving travellers and looking after the horses.)

On her side, Louise cleaned houses, took in laundry, sewed, and worked in the fields when the weather was fine. She interrupted her activities for only a short period after the birth of little Justin in February 1855. Bernadette brought the baby to her mother at work to be breastfed.

In autumn 1855, Lourdes was hit by a cholera epidemic. Bernadette, being more fragile than other members of her family, was affected. She recovered but was left with abdominal pain for the rest of her life.

The cereal harvest was poor and at the end of 1856 a vast famine occurred. This meant fewer opportunities for employment, a lower income and a very hard life for the Soubirous.

Bernadette's faith was real. Although she showed no outward signs of piety, she would often touch the beads of the rosary that she kept discretely in her pocket. She enjoyed reciting evening prayers with her family. At times, she even persuaded Jean-Marie out of his bed to join everybody in prayer. Before they went to sleep, she would invite Toinette to say a Hail Mary with her. Her faith consisted essentially in an intimate bond with God. But she felt an increasing need to strengthen and nurture that faith by receiving communion.

Bernadette was nearly thirteen. Yet all her desires, as legitimate as they were, were once again to be confined to the realm of dreams. Times were hard and were getting harder. The Soubirous had too many mouths to feed.

Aunt Bernarde offered to accommodate Bernadette at her own expense until spring, so that she could eat her fill. And indeed, Bernadette wanted for nothing. In return, she was asked to take care of her cousins. She did housework and sewing. She helped her aunt at the tavern that she ran. She returned home five or six months later without having been to school or to Catechism during that period.

Things were not improving for the Soubirous. It reached the point where they could no longer pay their rent. Exasperated by their repeated delays, their landlord served them notice of eviction.

In the "Cachot"

So they found themselves on the streets at the end of 1856 with no fixed employment and no money with which to rent a new place. During the short time available to him, François Soubirous looked for somewhere, however small, to house his family, but in vain. In desperation, he accepted the proposal of a cousin living at rue des Petits-Fossés: a single room, 3 meters by 4, giving onto an inner courtyard where hen manure was heaped. Known as "le Cachot" (the dungeon) because it was formerly a prison, it was insalubrious and therefore unused. And thus the former miller who was highly regarded by everyone, finally found refuge in a slum deemed unsuitable for criminals: an environment quite unfavourable to Bernadette's fragile health!

François continued to work at Maisongrosse and Cazenave. Louise worked when she was asked and Bernadette looked after her younger brothers on these occasions.

Although everyone did their best, life was very hard at the Cachot. At the end of spring 1857, the wet nurse from Bartrès asked whether she could take Bernadette during the summer to look after her sheep, and the Soubirous agreed. They were reluctant to see her leave but knew that food would be better and more substantial at the farm. And the air of Bartrès would be healthier than the stale atmosphere of the Cachot.

A promise is a promise

At the end of June 1857, Bernadette went to work as a shepherdess in Bartrès.

Each morning before leading the herd to pasture and in the evening once they were safely in their pen, she would help the maid with the children and with the housework.

This pace of life did not allow Bernadette to attend Catechism classes regularly with the children of the village as

Marie Laguës had promised. Bernadette did not hide her dissatisfaction. Mme Laguës felt a degree of guilt about this situation and tried to find a solution of her own. At night, before going to bed, she would read lessons from an old textbook and ask the young girl to repeat them several times without explaining their meaning. Bernadette was disconcerted by such a poor teacher who showed no tact or patience and asked of her underused memory feats that it was incapable of providing.

Both of them were so exasperated by this painful experience that it proved impossible to prolong it. Summer went by without Bernadette being authorized to leave the farm. When school resumed, Marie Laguës still refused to let her go.

Bernadette patiently endured the authoritarian personality of her nurse as well as the harsh working conditions that differed from those on which Marie Laguës and her parents had agreed. But she could no longer bear to be denied the right to attend school and Catechism. She decided to put an end to this situation. Her stay had initially been planned for just the summer but appeared to be extending indefinitely.

One Sunday in January 1858, Marie Laguës allowed Bernadette to visit her parents. She told them why she did not want to return to Bartrès and managed to convince them. As a result, she came back to the Cachot on January 28, 1858 and to the poverty of this cramped and unsanitary dwelling. But she also returned to a warm and loving family that gave her the strength to overcome the greatest hardships.

A pupil who did not neglect her duties

Bernadette was enrolled at the Hospice, a school run by the Sisters of Charity of Nevers,[1] which Toinette already attended regularly. From the outset, Bernadette displayed her strong desire to catch up in reading, writing and arithmetic, and showed a real ability for needlework. She obeyed the Sisters faultlessly and was always friendly to her classmates. Gifted at repartee, she never missed an opportunity to joke. Twice a week, Father Pomian, one of the three vicars of Father Peyramale, the Curate of Lourdes, gave Catechism lessons at the Hospice. His appraisal of Bernadette's knowledge in that area was categorical: "No idea of doctrine…"

On Thursdays (the weekly school holiday) and on the days her mother worked, Bernadette did the cooking and cleaning at the Cachot. On these occasions, she also looked patiently after her sisters and brothers to whom she always made herself available. She knew how to keep them busy, to entertain and comfort them whenever they were sad. But she was also severe when necessary and knew how to command obedience from them and from Toinette, who was not allowed to hang around with the local kids as she would have liked!

---

1. The Sisters of Charity of Nevers had opened a home at Lourdes for old and sick people without resources. They also ran a primary school for girls there.

Chapter II

When the invisible reveals itself

No wood for the fire

At the beginning of February 1858, work was still scarce and poorly paid. Despite all their efforts, the Soubirous were barely scraping a living. On the days when Louise was without work, she would go to the banks of the river Gave to collect the debris washed up by high water: bones, pieces of metal, rags… that she would sell to the local scrap merchant for a few coins. She also gathered dead wood to make bundles to sell after keeping some for the family. This is what she was about to do on February 11, 1858, having noticed that there was no more wood for the fire. Her two daughters were at home as it was a Thursday. Then a friend of the two girls, Jeanne Abadie, known as Baloum, arrived unexpectedly. She suggested that Louise stay with the younger boys at the Cachot: she would gladly accompany the sisters herself. Their mother agreed after having told Bernadette to wrap herself up well because it was cold.

Between the Gave and the rock

The rue des Petits-Fossés echoed with the clicks of clogs and cheerful conversations as the three girls walked towards the path going along the Savy canal[1]. They crossed the canal and headed to its confluence with the river Gave, common ground where poor people were allowed to gather wood. They arrived in front of the rock of Massabielle, which had many cavities including a large grotto at ground level with an oval-shaped niche above it; a wild rose bush grew at the base of that niche. The canal and a strip of sand and gravel behind it stood between the girls and the grotto.

They saw pieces of dry wood on the gravel and bits of bone inside the grotto. They decided to cross over. With one hand holding a basket and the other hitching up their skirts, Toinette and Baloum walked across. Bernadette was about to follow them but she first stopped to take off her stockings so that she would be able to warm her feet as soon as she had crossed. The others were already busy working.

From shock to rapture

Bernadette suddenly heard a sound like a gust of wind. She raised her eyes towards the niche where it apparently came from. According to her testimony,[2] she noticed at that moment "that a bunch of sticks and brambles were swaying… while everything around them was still." Inside

---

1. Water taken upstream from river Gave flowed down this canal to the Savy mill before rejoining the Gave downstream from Massabielle.
2. Mgr Trochu, *Sainte Bernadette, la Voyante de Lourdes*, Éd. Vitte, Lyon-Paris, 1953, p. 34.

the niche, she saw "a supernatural light" in which a "beautiful lady" appeared. She "seemed very young" and was approximately Bernadette's height (1.4 metres, 4.6 feet). She was wearing "a white dress, a blue girdle and a yellow rose on each foot." She was enveloped in "a white veil which covered her head, her shoulders and her arms, and almost reached the bottom of her dress."

At first, Bernadette had a feeling of fear, and couldn't believe her eyes: "I was afraid. I stepped back. I wanted to call the younger ones but I wasn't brave enough." "Thinking it was an illusion, I rubbed my eyes but to no avail, I kept seeing the same Lady." Indeed, Bernadette could not turn away from that beautiful face with its clear expression lit up by a gentle smile. But was "this" really coming from God? In order to make sure, she took out her rosary. If the Lady had been sent by the "Evil Spirit," she would certainly vanish at the first Hail Mary. Her fears disappeared when she saw the Lady make the sign of the cross in the most solemn and prayerful way she had ever seen. Bernadette began reciting her rosary. The Lady took hers and slipped the beads through her fingers one by one. Some moments later, the vision and its bright cloud disappeared.

Bernadette was still kneeling down, hands joined and eyes riveted to the niche, her face extremely pale. Toinette and Baloum who had been away looking for wood came back to the grotto at that moment. They had made their bundles and laid down their basket which was half-filled with debris. When they saw Bernadette on her knees, gazing at the grotto, they accused her of spending time in prayer instead of helping them. But Toinette was worried by her sister's paleness and feared the worst. She shared her fears with Baloum who replied: "If she was dead, she would be lying down."

Secret shared, secret revealed

When she came back to herself, Bernadette removed her other stocking and stood up. She hitched up her skirt and apron and crossed the canal. Then she put her stockings and clogs back on and started picking up dry sticks to add to her bundle.

The sound of the Angelus ringing brought the three girls back to reality: it was midday and they had to get back soon. All the way home, Bernadette remained silent, looking at the others out of the corner of her eye trying to find any sign that betrayed that they had also seen the Lady. She couldn't help asking:

"Didn't you see anything?"

"No we didn't. What about you?"

"Oh, no! If you have seen nothing, neither have I[1]."

Bernadette's simple question was enough to stimulate the curiosity of Toinette and Baloum who were fully determined to find out more. Bernadette had therefore seen something. As a sister and a friend they had the right to know. They swore they would keep the secret! Bernadette let herself be persuaded.

---

1. Mère Bordenave, *Sainte Bernadette, La Confidente de l'Immaculée*, Nevers-Saint-Gildard, 1912, p. 18.

She invited them to stop on the side of the road. Pricking up their ears, they waited to hear what she wanted to tell them. Then she declared that she had seen a beautiful young "Lady" dressed in white with a blue girdle and a yellow rose on each foot. And that she would love to see her again... They carried on walking, at a faster pace. Moments later, the two sisters left Baloum to get back to the "Cachot." In spite of her promise, Toinette couldn't hold her tongue and disclosed her sister's secret to her mother. Louise didn't hide her displeasure: "Woe is me! What are you saying?"

And turning to Bernadette who was silent, she said: "Your eyes misled you... it was probably a white stone that you saw."

"No," she replied firmly. "She has a beautiful face."

And her mother said in conclusion: "We must pray to God, maybe it's the soul of one of our family in purgatory[1]."

When the divine is manifested

The Lady seen by Bernadette was neither the fruit of her imagination, nor a soul missing her family. From February 11th to July 16th 1858, she appeared 18 times in the niche above the grotto of Massabielle. The urge to go to the strip of sand and gravel lying between the rock and the canal[1] would strike Bernadette very early in the

---

1. Mgr Trochu, p. 88.
2. The Savy canal had been filled in. The bed of the river Gave, which was very close to it (because of the confluence,) was moved back by several meters.

morning[1]. On arrival in front of the grotto, holding a lighted candle in one hand and her rosary in the other, she would kneel and pray in silence.

A few moments later, the Lady would appear in the midst of her brightness. Bernadette's face became extremely pale and was lit by a beaming smile. Her eyes gazed unswervingly at the niche. Her motionless body did not respond to any external phenomenon. She was unaware of the prick of a needle or of a candle's flame licking her hands. As soon as the Lady disappeared, she regained her colour, rose to her feet and went home oblivious to the feelings of admiration expressed towards her by an audience which grew daily more numerous.

Although there were elements of ritual to Bernadette's behaviour, it was also subject to certain exceptions. She sometimes talked or made signs to those around her. One day, the Lady asked her to go and drink water from the spring. People saw her walk to find that spring, enter the grotto, dig the ground and wash her face with and drink some of the water that had just spurted forth.

A message to deliver

Before and after Bernadette discovered the spring, the Lady spoke to her on several occasions. She gave her personal advice. She also gave her a message to deliver to the world and formulated requests directed to the clergy. Finally, she introduced herself:

---

1. At some occasions the Lady didn't manifest herself or appeared with a few hours' delay.

"I am the Immaculate Conception[1]."

Some essential points of that message were:

– do penance for the conversion of sinners;

– drink water from the spring and wash there;

– tell the priests to build a chapel and have people come in procession.

The Mother of God declared to her messenger: "I do not promise to make you happy in this world, but in the next."

Here are a few elements for reflection.

Penance means first of all to accept, in union with Christ's suffering, all the sorrows and difficulties of life.

The conversion of sinners is obviously the conversion of each one of us to complete and trusting surrender to a God whose love and mercy overflows.

To drink from the spring like Bernadette and wash oneself with its water means to rid ourselves of all personal and external obstacles which separate us from Jesus, the Living Water. A spring that leads us to the Light of the World, symbolized by the burning candle held by Bernadette.

To build a chapel means that each one of us needs to live as an authentic member of the Church. To come in procession means to come together from all nations and express our same and unique faith.

If Mary defined herself as the Immaculate Conception, it is to assure us that her intercession with her Son is powerful. Never touched by sin, she opens her motherly arms

---

1. Mother Bordenave, p. 48.

to us. She pledges to guide us in our steps towards conversion and sustain us in our struggle towards the next world where true happiness is promised to us as it was to Bernadette: a world where "Christ is sufficient."

Bernadette stands firm

These experiences were not easy for Bernadette. At first, her parents did not allow her to visit the grotto. But they knew their daughter well, and knew that she was unable to lie. She was clear-sighted enough to avoid being fooled by her imagination. She was simple and reserved enough to find no pleasure in drawing attention to herself by stage managing a false event. Besides, they knew she was determined to follow the Lady's instructions, which they also felt came from God. All these reasons led them to authorise what they had initially forbidden.

At school, she did not complain when her classmates made fun of her and when the sceptical Sisters strongly advised her to stop her ridiculous comedy.

She repeatedly endured questioning by the police, the judge, the public prosecutor and the mayor. She faced them without shame or embarrassment and with a firmness that was never dented. Whenever someone threatened to send her to jail if she refused to withdraw her statements, she immediately retorted: "That's fine! I will cost my father less and in prison you'll teach me Catechism." Or she said that the prison doors would need to be strong enough to stop her from escaping…

The clergy meditates

The local clergy did not react in the same reactionary way. The Curate of Lourdes, Father Peyramale wisely reserved judgement. Every day, he listened carefully to the testimonies of those who had witnessed the "apparitions", without giving his opinion. He did not authorise his three vicars to go to the grotto in order to avoid having their presence give weight to the facts. However, one vicar, Father Pomian, who was a chaplain at the Hospice and had heard Bernadette's confessions, allowed her to respond to the Lady's calls.

The first time that Bernadette came to Father Peyramale on behalf of the Lady and asked him to build a chapel, he challenged the beautiful stranger: if she really came from Heaven, she would make the wild rose bush in the niche bloom during that month of February! And she would reveal her name. In that case, he would believe Bernadette and her story, and obey the instructions conveyed by the young girl. At each of Bernadette's visits, Father Peyramale's incredulity gave way to more positive feelings. He appreciated her candour and her intuitive but solid faith. He knew the selflessness of her parents who in spite of their poverty refused the slightest favour of money or in kind. He knew that Bernadette was not attached to money either.

No, she was attracted neither by glory, profit or an easy life. Her unique desire was to stay in her mean Cachot surrounded by the warmth and love of her family and catch up with her education and Catechism.

The signs speak

Father Peyramale was able to appreciate Bernadette's qualities because he knew her better. Furthermore he noticed that the events at Massabielle had positive effects on the parishioners: they prayed more fervently, they lived in greater conformity with the gospel, goods were restored, forgiveness was granted, mass and services were attended more regularly, communion and confession were more frequently made... If only the wild rose bush would start to blossom and the Lady reveal her identity, nothing would prevent him from breaking his silence! But the branches, numbed by the winter cold, remained bare. A good lesson to remind the priest that God's work manifests itself in due time. And this time came on Thursday March 20th when, as we know, the Lady responded to Bernadette's appeals and designated herself as the "Immaculate Conception." Staggered by this revelation, Father Peyramale was then convinced that Bernadette spoke the truth and he wrote to his bishop to request the setting up of a commission of inquiry. This was done on November 17th, 1858. Let us leave this assembly to examine in its heart and conscience the actions and words of Bernadette and perform its investigation in the light of the most varied and most serious testimonies.

The crowd prays

We now return to the period following March 25. Bernadette saw the Lady only on April 3, which was Easter

Wednesday, and on July 16, the day she said farewell. Except on these two occasions, she did not return to Massabielle but spent her time doing her schoolwork and preparing her first communion which took place on June 3 in the Hospice chapel[1].

Despite her absence, more people kept coming to Massabielle from Lourdes, Bigorre and even abroad. These spontaneous pilgrims expressed their love to Mary Immaculate and told her their sorrows. They took water from the spring and drank it. Miracles were even reported: a hand with crippled fingers regaining form and movement, a paralysed child starting to walk, a blind man's eyes opening to light.

Yes, Mary was present at Massabielle. Those who gathered there to pray in silence or sing hymns had that conviction even before hearing the conclusions of the inquiry. Popular piety placed a plaster virgin and a few objects on a small altar: images of saints, rosaries, bowls of flowers and, in front of the niche, a wooden candle holder made by a carpenter. To facilitate access to the premises, the quarrymen[2] widened the steep footpath which descended to the grotto's entrance; they made a more gentle slope by adding bends. In front of the grotto, they created a more accessible area and built a small pool to make it easier to collect water.

_____

1. It is possible to visit this recently renovated chapel and the small museum of souvenirs set up in an adjoining room by the Sisters of Charity of Nevers.
2. Stonecutters working in quarries. This profession and that of millers was very common at Lourdes.

Massabielle had indeed become the privileged venue where all the children of the earth could express their faith and trust in their Mother.

Chapter III

When the truth becomes obvious

An exuberant fakery

Although Bernadette did not go to Massabielle any more, she was emulated in strange ways. Boys and girls saw luminous vapours in several recesses of the rock among which a lady, a group of cherubs, Saint Joseph, or one of the twelve apostles or saints from Paradise appeared. Some heard celestial melodies that sometimes turned into horrible cacophony. Young girls made an exhibition of themselves, playing the "Mother of Sorrows" with a great many sighs, tears and contortions, thus pretending to model themselves on Mary weeping as she held her dead Son in her arms. This exuberant behaviour was nothing more than fakery, or the imaginings of a few lunatics, and could only have a detrimental effect on the canonical enquiry. After discussing the matter with his bishop, Father Peyramale made an appeal to reason to all these fanciful individuals. By the end of summer, all the "visionaries" had disappeared.

The authorities are worried

The grotto and its surroundings had returned to the peaceful and prayerful atmosphere of the first days. But the huge crowds worried the mayor, Mr. Lacadé, the police superintendent Jacomet and the departmental prefect, who were in charge of public order and security. They considered that the worship taking place in front of the grotto could not be authorised whilst the Church did not recognize the events. The items that had been placed there needed to be removed urgently. Jacomet had them taken away. The mayor, the superintendent and the prefect set aside some time to find a way of putting a halt to the ever-increasing flow of people.

Lourdes, a thermal town?

Some time later, Mr Lacadé submitted to his two collaborators the idea that had occurred to him. As people were talking about healing brought about by the spring's water, the solution was to show that it possessed real qualities. So they ordered a pharmacist from Tribes, near Tarbes, to make a fake analysis. He declared the water to be rich in minerals. Its lightness was supposed to facilitate digestion. What an opportunity for the town of Lourdes! The spring was located in a common area and could therefore be exploited by the town and compete with Bagnères-de-Bigorre, Cauterets, and the other thermal spas in the region.

On June 8, Mr Lacadé issued an order that prohibited access to the grotto and the spring. A barricade was even built in front of the grotto on his instructions.

In addition to these decisions, the prefect wished to remove the source of these incidents: Bernadette. He ordered three medical examinations with the intention of sending the young girl to a lunatic asylum if she showed any mental disorder. Prior to these examinations, Father Peyramale ensured that he met with the three doctors appointed by the prefect. He told them that as long as he lived he would never allow a single hair on Bernadette's head to be touched. The doctors did not find any mental dysfunction in Bernadette. However they did not deny that she might have suffered from hallucinations. To reinforce their authority, they prescribed a period of rest.

In the meantime, on August 8th 1858, the mayor received the results of a counter-examination of the spring water analysis. A distinguished chemist, Mr. Filhol, professor at the Faculty of Science in Toulouse, declared that the water "did not contain any active substance that could give it particular therapeutic properties[1]." Other chemists later confirmed his conclusions. Lourdes would therefore never become a major thermal town to the great disappointment of Mr. Lacadé, who managed to make the best of it. The barricade was demolished before his eyes on October 5th 1858, on the order of Napoleon III himself [2]. Access to the grotto and the spring was again open to everyone, but only private worship was authorised until the commission of inquiry, which heard Bernadette for the first time on November 7th, announced their decisions.

---

1. Mother Bordenave, p. 75-76.
2. His Minister of Religion had passed on the order to the prefect who transmitted it to the mayor.

Intrusive visitors

The Soubirous had left the Cachot in September following Dr. Douzous' entreaties. He was more and more worried about Bernadette's frequent bouts of asthma. The doctor had emphasised the dangers of keeping their daughter, and the rest of the family in such an insalubrious environment. A few months later, François rented the watermill at Gras. It was unoccupied and located upstream from the Boly mill on the Lapaca river. He resumed his previous activity with renewed energy. One can imagine his satisfaction in relieving Louise from her hard work outdoors and the children's joy in having plenty of space at last. Not to mention Bernadette who had a room of her own in which she immediately placed a statue of the Virgin in prominence!

The prospect of an impending recognition of the events of Massabielle had attracted more crowds to the grotto but also to the Gras mill. As at the Cachot, people constantly came to question Bernadette about the apparitions and ask her to intercede for them in her prayers.

Father Peyramale had been aware for a long time of the urgent need to stop these intrusive visitors from disturbing the Soubirous in their work and taking up all Bernadette's time. He called on them and invited the family to adopt what seemed to him to be the only solution: Bernadette should become a boarder at the Hospice. Appreciating the good sense in this offer both for their daughter and for themselves, they eventually agreed. She would be taken in as an ill and destitute person. Although she was too old for school, she would be allowed to attend classes to improve her French. The thought of leaving the family she loved so much did not please Bernadette at all. Especially as since September 1859 she had had one more reason to be attached to them: Bernard-Pierre, her youngest brother was born and she was delighted to be his godmother. But listening to the voice of reason, she yielded to her parents' decision, on the specific condition that she could visit them twice a week and go to the grotto.

No spare time for Bernadette

So on July 15th 1860, Bernadette went to the Hospice as a boarder. Each day she attended class for a few hours. She helped take care of the sick in the infirmary to compensate for the free accommodation offered by the Sisters. She also helped to teach young girls to read and enjoyed entertaining them during break times. As she was attentive and applied in her studies, she made rapid progress in French. By 1860-1861, she was even able to write short texts quite well, though they still contained major spelling and grammar mistakes.

The religious education lessons given by Father Pomian and regularly followed by Bernadette since her confirmation (February 5, 1860) had enabled her to enrich her knowledge of Catechism. When she attended mass on Sundays at the parish church or when she prayed at the Hospice chapel, her calm and solemn face reflected a deep intimacy with the Lord. She was convinced that union with the loving and merciful God does not necessarily depend on painstaking mental gymnastics over the Mysteries of faith which is what she considered meditation to be. "I don't know how to meditate," she admitted. Yes, Mary had come to teach her that union with God is above all an exchange of love.

A faithful docility

She obeyed the Sisters unfailingly. Although they had assured Bernadette that they would spare her exhausting conversations with those who wanted to meet her, she agreed, in spite of her reluctance, to do so whenever the Sisters asked her to. The bell would ring a few times for her and she would discretely leave the classroom or wherever she was to walk to the parlour. She tried to reply kindly, often many times each day, to what were mostly the same questions as the day before.

Her natural docility did not alter her determination to see the rights of each and everyone respected. When she found herself unfairly criticised, she replied quickly and incisively. If for some reason the Mother Superior forgot to let her go when she was supposed to visit her parents or go to the grotto, Bernadette reminded her that she had made commitments: "It was a promise," she would say without losing her composure.

Tobacco, strawberries and crinoline

To her classmates, most of whom were younger than her, Bernadette was a good and cheerful friend with a real sense of humour. She was mischievous when she felt like it, as some of her classmates testified later. To bring her some relief from her bouts of asthma, the doctor told her to sniff tobacco. She always carried some in a box that she kept in her pocket. One day in class, she took out the box to breathe in the beneficial fragrance. On that occasion, she stealthily passed on a few pinches of tobacco to classmates nearby. A series of sneezes followed. And everybody had the giggles.

The following anecdote is even more delightful: one day in June, Bernadette was attending a sewing class on the first floor. Through the window, she was contemplating a patch of strawberries right below, alongside the vegetable garden. The fruits were ripening and the blazing sunlight enhanced their sweet fragrance, giving her the irresistible desire to eat some. Access to the garden was forbidden when there was no specific reasons to go there, so she had to come up with an excuse. Bernadette took advantage of a few moments break between two classes to elaborate a plan. She knew she could count on the complicity of her friend, Julie Garros, so she whispered in her ear: "I'm going to throw my shoe into the garden… you will fetch it and bring back strawberries." And it was done, for the greatest pleasure of both girls. Who would dare criticise Bernadette for her teenage playfulness? Or for trying to look smart by enlarging her skirt to resemble a crinoline or putting a piece of wood in her corset to give more volume to her breast?…

The bishop is shaken and the doctor astounded

On December 7th 1860, Bernadette was summoned for final questioning by the commission of inquiry, chaired by Mgr Laurence himself. After watching her repeat the gestures of the Virgin who declared herself to be the Immaculate Conception, the bishop could not hold back tears of emotion. His innermost conviction was well-founded. However, he gave himself some time for reflection before taking the decision that would bind the Church. On January 18th 1862, he issued a pastoral letter in which he recognised the authenticity of the apparitions of Massabielle.

In March, Bernadette contracted pneumonia and was confined to her bed. Repeated coughing and severe asthma attacks resulted in such violent fits of breathlessness that the nursing Sister and her assistant had to carry her to the window so that she could breathe. She told them between two moans: "Open up my chest!" On the evening of April 27th, the doctor said there was no hope for Bernadette. Her parents were invited to see her a last time and they could not hold back their tears. The Sisters and the boarders of the Hospice took turns to pray at her bedside. During the night, Father Pomian came to administer the last rites. She opened her eyes and with a reedy voice asked for a sip of water from the grotto. Right after, she told the Sister sitting up with her that she was completely healed: "I felt," she said "a mountain coming off my chest.[1]"

The next morning, the doctor arrived for his regular visit. The Sister who showed him in asked him to go to the parlour. He thought he would find the Mother Superior

---

1. P. A. de Nevers, p. 304.

coming to announce the death of the patient. One can imagine his surprise to be welcomed by Bernadette in person.
She was still weak but smiling. She had been completely
cured of her illness, but not from asthma which persisted.

The parish priest opens his building site

After Mgr Laurence had issued his pastoral letter,
Father Peyramale had not been idle. He created a large
building site that would establish pilgrimage at Massabielle. The town sold all the area surrounding the grotto
to the diocese of Tarbes and Father Peyramale purchased
several plots of land on each side of the canal. Established
as "project manager" by his bishop, he had the grotto
cleared of all the material accumulated by the overflows
of the river Gave. He had a small pool constructed to
collect water from the spring and make it more accessible. After supervising the diversion of the canal, he had
the ground levelled and faced. He also supervised the
construction of a thick granite wall as a protection
against the rise of the water level. As for the chapel
requested by the Virgin, this would be a beautiful church
built on the rock. First a crypt would be constructed
which would form its base.

François Soubirous was one of the first workmen to
wield spade and pick-axe on the site levelled for the crypt's
construction. His poor ability as a manager meant that he
was unable to make a living at the Gras mill. Instead he
was hired to work on Father Peyramale's building site.

When indulgence reaches its limits

While the work continued at Massabielle, Bernadette gradually filled in the gaps in her education and provided assistance as needed in the infirmary or with the youngest children. She found the visits to the parlour more and more of a chore. She detested the insensitivity of those who, considering her to be a living relic, wanted to take a souvenir of her away with them, wanted to cut a lock of her hair.

Those who tried to slip a coin into her hand as they left were requested to put the money in the pot for the poor. To the Sisters who asked her whether her asthma caused her much discomfort, she answered that the attacks were no more unbearable than all "this hugging and kissing".

Two-penny photos

She also had to endure another chore : the taking of photographs. Father Peyramale had had the idea of producing thousands of copies of portraits of her, which would be sold to finance the works at Massabielle. On a number of occasions, Bernadette had to attend, against her will, lengthy sitting sessions which annoyed her intensely. Visitors who had bought a copy of the photograph would ask her to sign it. All she would write is "pp Bernadette" meaning 'priez pour Bernadette' (pray for Bernadette). And when she learned that these photographs were sold for two pennies, she laughed and said "that's all I'm worth!"

Her twice weekly visits to her parents and to the grotto were consolation for her heart as well as her spirit. In July

1863 she had the satisfaction of seeing her family take up residence in a decent home at last: the Lacadé mill, bought by Father Peyramale who rented it to them at a very low price.

A statue worth its weight in gold

If the photos weren't worth more than tuppence, the statue of the Virgin, commissioned by two rich sisters[1] would cost 7000 gold francs. It was placed in the niche where Mary appeared to Bernadette and was made by a well-known sculptor, Joseph-Hugues Fabisch. Before he started his work, he came to Lourdes to meet Bernadette. He asked her questions about the Lady, her age, her height, how she was dressed, the expression on her face. And also, about her attitude at each visit, notably the time when she specified "I am the Immaculate Conception". Fabisch was captivated and went back to Lyon impatient to begin chiselling away at his immaculate white block of Carrara marble.

---

1. The Lacour sisters, from Chasselay in the Rhône department of France.

Chapter IV

Lights and shadows

A meeting which opens the door to the future

A few days later the Bishop of Nevers, Mgr Forcade, paid a visit to the Sisters of Charity in his role as their Superior[1]. Having expressed the wish to meet Bernadette, the Mother Superior took him to the kitchens where she was busy peeling carrots. Indicating her with her eyes, Mother Superior whispered in his ear :

"That's it!"

The Bishop was not satisfied with this brief interview. After the meal he requested a meeting alone with Bernadette. He asked her to relate what had happened at Massabielle, which she did in very good French. He then wished to ask her about any eventual religious vocation she may have. Not daring to broach the subject too directly, he first asked her :

"So you are no longer a child. Maybe you would be happy to find [a job for yourself] away from here?"

---

1. The Sisters of Charity and Christian instruction of Nevers had their mother house in Nevers. As their congregation had not received recognition from the diocese, it was placed under the management of Mgr Forcade.

"Ah, not at all, what an idea!"

"Well, then why don't you become a Nun? Have you thought about it?"

"It's impossible Monsignor. You know that I am poor. I would never be able to raise the dowry."

Having understood the argument which stopped Bernadette from admitting her vocation, which he believed she felt, he hurried to remove the impediments

"But, my child, we also sometime accept poor young women as nuns, when they have a real vocation."

The generosity of his words touched Bernadette. However she also had the feeling that she herself was an obstacle to any request for admission

"But Monsignor, the ladies that you take without dowry are clever and wise and they repay you like that... But I, I know nothing and am good at nothing!"

The Bishop replied, with an amused smile,

"Earlier, in the kitchen, I noticed you were good at... peeling carrots. In religion, we will know how best to use you, indeed in the Novitiate we will complete your education."[1]

Everything was said. It was, for her, the opportunity for inner contemplation. And for the prelate, the end of a promising conversation that he hurried to relate to the Mother Superior. She declared herself inclined to accept Bernadette should she request admission. But she decided to stop the Sisters from influencing Bernadette with their

---

1. Some extracts from this interview, according to Mgr Trochu "Sainte Bernadette…" p. 34.

words, because she knew that persuasion wasn't the most efficient way of attracting a girl of her calibre to the convent.

Bernadette says "yes, but..."

The artist had not been idle in his workshop, since returning to Lyon. Towards the end of March 1864, he gave a last chisel blow to the sculpture and then he took it to Lourdes, arriving on the 30th. His first visit was to Father Peyramale who, at his request, accompanied him to the Hospice to get the impressions of Bernadette in his presence. Having asked to meet her, they were taken to the parlour. After she had arrived, he removed the statue from its well-padded wooden box and placed it on a side-board. As soon as they saw her enter the room, the priest asked her, as he pointed to the statue, the question which was burning their lips :

"Did it look like that?"

"Yes, it looked like that" she answered with an evasive tone. And then, after thinking for a moment,

"It's very beautiful but its not Her... Oh no! The difference is like the Earth to the Sky."[1]

Rejoicing

Despite its imperfections, the pure marble statue was placed in the niche where the Virgin had appeared. On

---

1. Mère Bordenave, p. 95.

April 4th, a procession of 20 000 people carrying banners
and chanting hymns gathered in front of the parish
church. The long cortège marched through the town and
assembled on the land which had been recently cleared
around the grotto. Mgr Laurence, surrounded by more
than 400 priests, removed the veil which had been cove-
ring the statue and blessed it. "It seems to us that Mary
is still here," he said, "and that we see her as Bernadette
saw her."[1] Is there any pilgrim to Lourdes who doesn't
share the opinion of the prelate?

Tears and suffering

There was one man, in the front row of the delirious
crowd, who felt more pain than joy : Fabisch. He had taken
Bernadette's critical opinion as a personal blow. As soon as
the statue was raised to its niche, he was struck by an even
more painful blow : "I have to speak," he admitted, "of one
of the greatest sadnesses of my life...that which I felt when
I saw my statue in place, illuminated by a reflected
light...which completely changed the expression."[2]

The sculptor was not the only person who did not
share the general joy on that day. Father Peyramale was
confined to his bed by a fever which was a severe as it was
sudden. As for Bernadette, she had not left the Hospice : a new asthma attack? Or a measure taken by the
Mother Superior to spare her an emotionally draining

---

1. Mère Bordenave, p. 96-97.
2. Joseph Fabisch, "Mémoire Autographe", 1878.

encounter – or to preserve her from the pride which the over-enthusiastic admiration of the crowds may have provoked in her?

For whatever reason, she who had seen the Immaculate Conception with her own eyes and he who had believed in her word as messenger, were deprived of the satisfaction of seeing her effigy placed where the entire world could come and venerate it. The unfortunate creator of the work, who was well and truly present, was no less disenchanted.

The Mother Superior says "yes, but..."

Bernadette had been kept away from this manifestation in honour of the Queen of Heaven. But her image remained well and truly alive in her memory. And even if she hadn't seen her since, she often heard her speak with the ear of her heart. She had the impression, on that day, that she encouraged her to take the decision which would close this long period of contemplation. That evening, she asked to meet with the Mother Superior, to inform her that she felt called to enter her congregation. The Mother Superior reserved her answer for August 15th. She then told her that she had been accepted but that it had to be confirmed by the Superior General of the Sisters of Charity of Nevers. Furthermore, she wouldn't do her novitiate at Lourdes but at Nevers, the mother house. The Mother Superior there required her to be restored to full health before she would welcome her.

Relaxation and Affection

What better way to recover and gain in strength than a stay in a charming village, far from the agitation of the town and curious stares? This is what one of Bernadette's cousins, Jeanne Védère of Momères, suggested to her, when she came to visit on October 4th. Bernadette accepted the invitation without hesitation. She was at last going to have a real holiday, in a warm family environment! Her Mother Superior allowed her to leave after having been assured that Doctor Peyramale, brother of the priest of Lourdes, and doctor at Momères, would intervene should she suffer a serious asthma attack.

The stay was so pleasant that it was extended from its original duration of one week to a month and a half.

At the school of life

On November 19th, when she returned to Lourdes, Bernadette had the pleasant surprise of learning that she had been admitted to Nevers. At the Hospice, although she was not actually considered as a postulant, she participated more intensely in community life.

Is there any need to mention that her favourite moments were when she was with her parents or could visit her grotto? Her parents, indeed, needed the support of their daughter when they buried their poor Julien on February 1st 1865, aged not yet ten years old. Her dear little brother who she had so often cradled in her arms and looked after when her mother was not there! She became even more affectionate towards Toinette and the two boys, who were also very affected by the death. Less than a year had passed when the last daughter that Louise brought into the world died, shortly after birth. Bernadette helped them to find comfort in Christian hope and the thought that they had a fifth little intercessor in Heaven.

The reasons of wisdom

Bernadette felt useful at the Hospice, especially with the children and the sick who were particularly fond of her. She appreciated the cordial sentiments of the Sisters and her companions, a number of whom she considered as friends. Her regular visits to her parents and to the grotto provided her with real affection and spiritual support. Yes, for her Lourdes was her cradle, the place of all her attachments, the place where she wished to continue to live and to die. But there were still these visits which tired her and hindered her worship. And there was also the special attention that was focused on her, diametrically opposed to the simplicity that she had deliberately chosen. If she were to be able to consecrate herself fully to the Lord, she was convinced that she needed to separate herself from what she loved the most in the world : her family and her grotto.

Although Bernadette had been forbidden to be present when the statue was blessed, she did have the joy of attending the inauguration of the crypt, presided by Mgr Laurence. The ceremony was grandiose and the crowd, the like of which had never been seen, was as dense on the other bank of the Gave as it was on the space which had been cleared near the grotto. In the evening, a good number of people who hadn't been able to see Bernadette during the ceremony came knocking at the Hospice gates. When faced with the demands of the crowd who threatened to storm the building if they weren't given access to the "seer", the Mother Superior had her walk the length of the gallery, where she was visible to all. Bernadette complied, all the time muttering that the Mother Superior was exhibiting her "like a cow at a fair". This episode, which she submitted to out of obedience, strengthened her resolve to leave Lourdes.

The obligations of the heart

As the improvements in her health persisted, the date for her departure was set for July 4th 1866. The day before, she said her goodbyes to her dear grotto in the company of the Mother Superior. She knelt before the statue and didn't take her eyes off it. The Mother Superior heard her murmur, sobbing: "Oh, my Mother, my Mother, how can I leave you!" She stood to kiss the rock and dry her tears. The Mother Superior, herself moved by the scene, tried to console her : "Why do you make yourself so sad? Don't you know that the Holy Virgin is everywhere and that everywhere she will be your Mother?"

"Oh yes! I know," she replied with a sigh, "but the grotto was my Heaven".[2] Then the Mother Superior accompanied her to the Lacadé mill, where she left her to

---

1. Mère Forestier, P. A. Nevers, p. 218.

have her last meal with her family. We can imagine the emotional intensity of that evening, and the tears shed by all at this painful moment of separation.

The next day, Bernadette was ready to leave with four travelling companions. Nobody had slept well at the Soubirous. In the early hours of the morning, neither parents nor children could resist their need to see her one more time. A few moments before the car that was to take them to Tarbes station left, they went to the Hospice. They wanted to talk to her, to tell her again how much they loved her, remind her that she was in their prayers. But when they found themselves in her presence, the emotion was too much, they couldn't say a single word. They could only sigh, cry and hold her to their bosom, one after the other, to kiss her again and again. Bernadette wanted to put an end to this concerto of laments which drained her of what courage and strength she had left :

"It's all very well you crying, I can't stay here for ever".[1]

One last look, one last kiss and the travellers sank in to the car which set off with a deafening roar.

---

1. P. O. Nevers, p. 810.

Photo captions

I. Bernadette Soubirous.

II. François Soubirous (1807-1871), Bernadette's father.

III. Louise Soubirous, née Castérot (1825-1866), Bernadette's mother. She died aged 42 on December 8th 1866, the year that Bernadette left Lourdes (on July 4th).

IV. Bernadette Soubirous at Lourdes.

V. Bernadette Soubirous at Lourdes.

VI. Father Marie-Dominique Peyramale, priest of Lourdes at the time of the apparitions in Febraury 1858. First ecclesiastical recipient of the message from the Virgin at Massabielle, which he heard directly from Bernadette's mouth : "Que soy era immaculada councepciou", "I am the Immaculate Conception". Destroyed by the construction work on the new church, he died on September 8th 1877 (day of the Nativity of the Virgin Mary).

VII. The Mother Superior of the Lourdes Hospice with Bernadette.

VIII, IX, X. Bernadette.

XI. Page of Bernadette's writings – 28th December 1858.

XII. Saint-Pierre church, the parish church of Lourdes in 1858, destroyed in 1905.

XIII. Stained glass window representing the 1st apparition of the Virgin to Bernadette on February 11th 1858. At the base of the window we can read "Donation from the parish of Sainte-Eulalie of Montpellier, 1873".

XIV. Statue of Bernadette with lambs.

XV. Statue de Bernadette with roses.

XVI. The rosary which lay in her hands for 30 years in her coffin.

© Sanctuaires de Notre-Dame de Lourdes/EURL Basilique du Rosaire.

I

II

IV

© Sanctuaires de Notre-Dame de Lourdes - EURL Basilique du Rosaire.

V

80. — LOURDES.
Monseigneur
Peyramale
curé de Lourdes.

VI

© Sanctuaires de Notre-Dame de Lourdes - EURL Basilique du Rosaire.

VII

VIII

IX

VIRON

X

marie marie marie marie

marie marie marie marie

marie marie marie ma

marie marie marie ma

marie marie marie marie

marie marie marie m

marie marie marie

marie marie marie

marie marie marie ma

marie marie marie ma

Bernadette Soubirous. 20 Decembre 1858

XII

XIII

SAINTE BERNADETTE

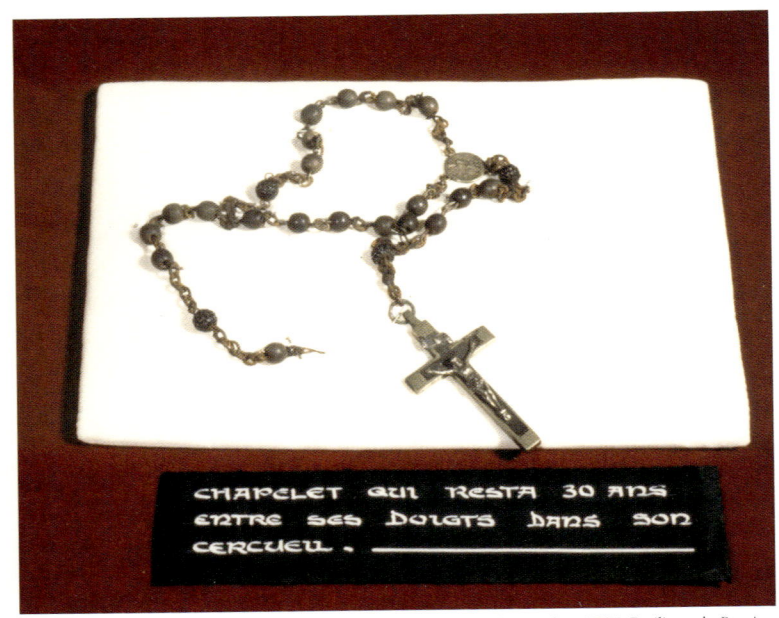

CHAPELET QUI RESTA 30 ANS
ENTRE SES DOIGTS DANS SON
CERCUEIL. _____

© Sanctuaires de Notre-Dame de Lourdes - EURL Basilique du Rosaire.

Chapter 5

Heart in the Heavens, feet on the ground

Once and for all

The five travellers arrived at Nevers at 10.30pm on Saturday July 7th. A car drove them to their destination: the Saint Gildard convent[1]. Only two or three Sisters were there to welcome them and make them some supper. Bernadette and her two companions were taken to the dormitory for novices and postulants.

The next morning, the three new arrivals were received by the Mother Superior, her assistants and the Novice Mistress, Mother Vauzou, under whose direction they were to be placed. With Bernadette's agreement, as she had come there to "hide herself", it was agreed that visits to the parlour would be restricted to only unavoidable cases. To rid her of any feeling of pride concerning the apparitions, she was formally forbidden to discuss the subject with any Sister. She was invited to tell the story the next morning in the presence of the Sisters of the three homes of the Order in the town. Once only. Once and for all.

---

1. So called because it had been built ten years earlier on the ruins of the Saint Gildard priory.

After mass, they showed her round the convent. In the early afternoon, she was taken to the novices hall where the Mother Superior invited her to speak in front of a large audience (around 300 Sisters). Without hesitation, she told the complete story of the apparitions and answered all the questions that were asked of her with clarity and precision.

Take comfort without forgetting

This first day had been full for her, but exhausting. If she felt happy to be finally able to live the secluded life that she desired, she could not stop herself from thinking about those who she had left behind : her father who could never bear to be far from her; her mother who risked a deterioration in her already fragile health due to her sadness; her dear Toinette, her Jean-Marie and Bernard-Pierre, her godson, who she would not see grow up. And her grotto, which she had found so difficult to leave! And her Sisters of the Hospice, her friends... Yes, Bernadette cried, as did her companion : "Léontine and I," she admitted, "spent much of Sunday crying."[1] This state of sadness would diminish each day for Bernadette, as she had discovered a place which afforded her peace. At the bottom of the garden reserved for novices stood a statue of a smiling virgin holding out her hands. She was entitled "Notre Dame Les Eaux" (Our Lady of the Water), because a

---

1. Mère Bordenave, *Sainte Bernadette, La Confidente de l'Immaculée,* p. 119.

spring flowed from beneath her feet, which was used to water the garden : a spring, like in Massabielle!

Bernadette was welcomed with happiness by the entire community. But this did not stop her from exposing her true feelings in a letter to the Sisters of the Hospice : "Pray for me when you go to the grotto. That is where you will find me in spirit, attached to the foot of the rock that I love so..."[1]

An enthusiastic member of the community...

To her great joy, Mother Vauzou gave Bernadette the name of her patron saint : she became Sister Marie-Bernard. She partook of all the exercises of novitiate: explanatory lessons about the Holy Rule, Holy Writings, doctrine, but also French and arithmetic. She was always friendly, very lively during breaks, and also ready to listen, console, offer advice... She filled her spare time with needlework, notably embroidery.

At the hours of prayer, she displayed real devotion according to those who saw her : "When she recited the rosary," noted a novice from her class, "you would have said that she saw the Holy Virgin like at Lourdes."[2]

Meditative, Bernadette? Certainly. But without the least affectation. Indeed, she did not hesitate to be scathing of the pretentious airs taken by certain to appear more

---

1. Letter dated 20.7.1866 to the Sisters of the Hospice of Lourdes, Archives of Saint Gildard.
2. Sister L Cloris, P. O. Nevers, p. 1101.

pious. On one occasion, a novice was walking in front of her, head lowered and eyes closed and was being guided, so as not to fall, by a neighbour who was holding her hand. Bernadette called to her, "why are you closing your eyes when we should be keeping them open?"[1]

With regards to the development of her spiritual life through reading we have little information, with the exception of her own testimony. She liked to read the Passion, about which she said, "It touches me more when I read it than when it is preached to us."[2]

Bernadette was an enthusiastic member of the community!

...who keeps her feet on the ground

Concerning the life of the saints, she rejected works of edification, where they were presented as being "so celestial that it tends to discourage us". A lucid observation that we are inclined to share. And to clarify : "The contemplation of their total triumph teaches me nothing : it is the vision of their battle that teaches me to fight."[3]

Yes, she had understood that sainthood does not necessarily consist of being the object of extraordinary acts, but much more than that, is an invitation to seek to live the evangelical message to the best of our abilities. This is the objective she set herself in her daily observance of the

---

1. Sister E. Marcillac, P. Nevers, p. 150.
2. H. Lasserre, *Notre Dame de Lourdes*, Lethielleux, Paris, 1869, p. 270.
3. *Idem*, p. 268.

Rules of the Congregation. She counted on her Superiors to help her improve her character, which she herself defined as "very bad".

In Mother Vauzou she was to find a useful support to guide her on the route to "humility, mortification, the spirit of sacrifice by all means."[1]

These means? Those used at the time : fighting pride with exercises of public humiliation : a hurtful word, the obligation to kneel in the novice room to kiss the floor... Mother Vauzou didn't hesitate to show a certain affection for Bernadette when, towards the end of August 1866, a particularly violent asthma attack confined her to her bed. Mother Vauzou asked her novices to pray for her recovery : "We are not worthy of possessing her, but we must implore the Heavens...."[2]

At death's door

After showing a slight improvement, Bernadette was again the victim of breathlessness, which aggravated the painful coughing up of blood, the first symptoms of her being afflicted by tuberculosis. On October 25th, the community's physician, Doctor Saint-Cyr, predicted that she wouldn't last the night. The chaplain came to administer the Last Rites, which she received for the second time.

But before leaving for this "other world", where she was promised happiness, she wished to make her vows.

---

1. Mère Bordenave, p. 120.
2. Mère Bordenave, p. 126.

She wanted to wear the uniform of her dear Sisters of the Charity of Nevers where Mary had led her. Permission was granted and Mgr Forcade decided to personally receive her vows. As she was too weak to pronounce them, he spoke on her behalf, asking her to accept each article by saying Amen.

We can imagine the sadness of her friends when they saw the Mother Superior place the veil over her head and Mother Vauzou place the crucifix in her hand and lay the Holy Rule on her bed. No sooner had the Bishop left, Bernadette opened her eyes, and murmured with a smile, "I shan't die tonight." Then she fell peacefully asleep. Around four in the morning, when the nursing Sister who was sitting with her was expecting the worst, she said to her, in a stronger voice "I feel better. God didn't want me. I went to the door and he said to me: "Go away, its too early." The whole of Saint Gildard seemed revived when they awoke to learn that she was still of this world.

Her convalescence was quite long. Bernadette used the time that she was bedridden for her needlework and to read the texts recommended to her by Mother Vauzou.

By mid-November she had regained enough strength to walk in the corridors and attend mass in the gallery of the chapel. It is whilst in this still-weakened state that she learnt of the death of her mother. The pain was such that she fainted in the midst of a crying fit. But she was comforted to learn that her mother had been called by the Lord on December 8th, the day of the Immaculate Conception!

Against a background of bitterness

After her recovery, Bernadette resumed the tasks of a novice. Her vows, taken *in articulo mortis* would have to be retaken at the date specified by the Holy Rule. Mother Vauzou's behaviour towards Bernadette changed. Under the pretext that her novice had received exceptional graces, she wanted to take her even further along the road to "perfection". She became more and more cold towards her. A number of her companions speak of her hardness towards her, the dry tone with which she addressed her, her tendency to annoy her. An attitude which, in fact, later she was to admit to herself: "Every time I had something to say to her, I was driven to address her with bitterness."[1]

These rebuffs were difficult for Bernadette to bear, who confessed one day to a Sister, "I am boiling inside," indicating her heart, "we would be worth nothing if were weren't capable of controlling ourselves".[2]

An "inner garden" which is not to be seen

What irritated Mother Vauzou about Bernadette was her refusal to completely confide in her, as she encouraged her novices to do. "Don't have secrets from me, unless it concerns the confession,"[3] she would tell them. At Lourdes, Bernadette had had Mary herself as her first Novice Mistress,

---

1. P. A. Nevers, p. 1123 (Sœur L. Villaret).
2. Sœur Marthe du Rais, P. A. Nevers, p. 1342.
3. E. Guynot, *Sainte Bernadette, Souvenirs Inédits*, Éd. du Cerf, Paris, 1978, p. 86.

and she had opened her heart and taught her trust that of her Son, and to start to live, from then on, in that other world where God alone is enough. And herein lies the source of what vexed Mother Vauzou. This notary's daughter, whose authority and ability to train good novices was unquestioned, was experiencing failure for the first time. The simple daughter of a ruined miller refused to yield her "inner garden". And yet, she was one of her best novices, loved by the entire community, known and venerated throughout the world.

Bernadette suffered from the attitude of her Mistress. But she interpreted it as the instrument of a particular grace, inviting her to make vigorous progress, without doubt, on the road to true happiness. In fact she was already well placed on that road to which humility leads. Some of her companions have, indeed, spoken of the poor idea that she had of herself. On day, during break time, standing between the two tallest novices, she said "Look at me! How could I think myself important given my small size?" When she learnt that the price of her photos, which had been widely reprinted, was reduced to 10 centimes, she burst out laughing at seeing herself at half price.

On another occasion, a postulant who had arrived at Saint-Gildard two days earlier, was complaining that she had yet to be introduced to her. A young Sister said to her, "Bernadette? Here she is!" The novice didn't hide her astonishment at the sight of this small and modest looking girl. "That?" Adopting the same tone, Bernadette answered "But yes, Mademoiselle, that's all it is!"[1]

---

1. Mère Bordenave, p. 130.

Chapter 6

To love and to serve

The use of prayer

Once she had recovered, Bernadette resumed her activities as a novice in preparation for her profession of vows. Her resolutions, which she had noted during the days of preparatory retreat, are a programme for life : "Live for God alone, for God everywhere, for God always. Only look for God alone in any thing, God everywhere, God always."[1]

On October 30th, 1867 she made her profession for one year.

The same evening, according to custom, the Mother Superior, in the presence of the Bishop and the entire community, distributed their duties to the newly professed...with the exception of Bernadette, who was to bear the name of Sister Marie-Bernard definitively. Mgr Laurence turned towards the Mother Superior and, feigning surprise, said :

"And Sister Marie-Bernard?"

"Monsignor, we are in a quandary : she is good at nothing."

"And so?"

---

1. *Les Écrits de Bernadette*, Sœurs de la Charité de Nevers, p. 253.

"If you have no objection, we will try and find use for her here, assisting the Nursing Sister. That is all she knows how to do."[1]

Remembering their encounter at Lourdes, he asked Sister Marie-Bernard

"Are you capable of carrying bowls of herbal tea, peeling vegetables?"

"I will try", she replied, with a slight amused smile which answered his own.

And to put an end to the conversation, he said :

"I charge you with the duty of prayer."[2]

Velvet Glove and Iron Hand

Bernadette took up her role as assistant nurse, under the orders of Sister Marthe. All those who were treated by her were unanimous in describing her delicate touch, her gentleness, her kindness, her affection, her capacity to console and to encourage. And, not least her happiness, which was contagious. When she had the time, she liked to climb to the infirmary on the second floor where the secular patients were treated. "She plumped up my pillow," said one of them, "mopped my brow, and held my hand with the tenderness of a real sister or a mother."[3]

Sister Marthe's health was deteriorating. Sometimes she herself had to take to her bed. Bernadette took on her responsibilities, following the prescriptions of Doctor Saint-Cyr.

1. Mère Bordenave, p. 136.
2. P. O. Nevers, p. 1297.
3. E. Guynot, *Souvenirs inédits*, p. 152.

The friendliness and sensitivity of Sister Marie-Bernard did not however mean that she could not be firm when she needed to be. One day, a young postulant was instructed by her to stay tucked up in bed. She made the most of a moment where Sister Marie-Bernard was busy elsewhere to pick up a prayer book. When her hands and forearms were seen to be out of bed, holding her book, it was taken from her and placed it out of reach, and Sister Marie-Bernard did not hide her annoyance : "And there you have it, a fever caused by disobedience!"[1]

An example, amongst many, which demonstrates that for Sister Marie-Bernard true devotion knows to never take precedence over the responsibility of the moment : such as that of a patient to obey the orders of their nurse.

Far from sight, close to the heart

Despite being kept busy at the Infirmary, Sister Marie-Bernard forgot neither her home town nor her family. She wrote regularly to Toinette, and was saddened that she did not know her husband, Joseph Sabathé. Through her she addressed the entire family : "I ask you to embrace them all on my behalf. Remember me to the children (brothers and cousins). Tell them to be good and to say a little "Hail Mary" for me, especially when they are at my dear grotto… My health is perfectly good… I am happy in all aspects. I close by embracing you affectionately. I ask my

---

1. Mère Bordenave, p. 140.

little [Bernard] Pierre (eight and a half) to give my father three big kisses from me."[1]

One year later, in May 1869, she was saddened by the departure of the Mother Superior and one of her assistants for Lourdes. As she could not accompany them, she asked them to pay a visit to her father at the Lacadé Mill (which he now owned) and her brothers, her sister and her brother-in-law who all lived with him.

Sister Marthe's illness was heading towards a fatal outcome. Sister Marie-Bernard was named as the head of the infirmary. Happily her health was steadily improving. And she needed to be robust when, in autumn 1870, as the Prussians were at the gates of the town, a military ambulance was based at Saint Gildard. This resulted in an increase in work for her, caused by the arrival of injured soldiers. Not for too long, however, as the armistice was signed on January 28th 1871.

It was just as the danger was at its most imminent that François Soubirous had planned to visit Nevers. Bernadette immediately wrote to Toinette to dissuade him. "I would also be very happy to see him. Tell him, however, not to set off. If by misfortune, anything bad should happen to him during the journey, I would blame myself for the rest of my life".[2]

"I come to weep with you"

During this year of 1871, whilst France found peace again, the Soubirous family had to bear great sadness : the

---

1. Letter to Marie (=Toinette). Saint-Gildard Archives.
2. Letter dated December 25th 1870. Saint-Gildard Archives.

death of the Sabathés' first two children, of François Soubirous and Aunt Lucile.[1]

At each of these sad occasions, Sister Marie-Bernard was quick to write to her family to share their sadness and to console them. This strong passage from her letter to Toinette after the death of her father and her daughter goes right to our hearts : "It pleased Our Lord to take from us what was the dearest thing in the world, our dear and much loved father. I come to weep with you... I have taken a large part of the pain that your heart of a mother has experienced... I end, my much loved sister, by embracing you all most affectionately; meet me at the foot of the cross, that is where we will find strength and courage."[2]

Sister Marie-Bernard also wanted to share her pain with Jean-Marie, who had entered the Brothers of Christian Instruction, and with Bernard-Pierre, who was being educated by the Fathers of Garaison. She cried with them, without neglecting her responsibilities as eldest sister, by inviting them to fulfil their duty and to pray for the living and the dead of the family.

Private conversation with the Lord

Doctor Saint-Cyr had total confidence in Sister Marie-Bernard and all her patients held her in esteem and considered it a privilege to be nursed by her. But her repeated

---

1. Respectively, February 12th and August 29th for little Bernard and Bernadette, March 4th and 16th for François and Lucile.
2. Letter to Mary, 9 March 1871.

asthma attacks and her painful coughing fits provoked by the unstoppable progression of her tuberculosis meant that she could no longer continue as a nurse. She was moved to the sacristy in the first days of 1874.

This new role meant that she could spend long moments in front of the tabernacle. In private conversation with Christ who had overcome death, she listened to him speak to her heart, and confided in him all the intentions of her family. She always begged for the intercession of Mary, before her altar, for those who had asked for her prayers, without forgetting the sinners for whom she had been invited to pray at the Massabielle grotto. She took particular care of the altar cloth and the floral decoration, with as much taste as pleasure. During these sacristan activities, she lived her union with God with a more affective familiarity, as a group of novices were witness : one Christmas day, when she took the baby Jesus to place him in the crib that they had made together, she spoke these words that remained engraved on their memories : "You must be very cold, my poor little Jesus, in a stable in Bethlehem. They were heartless, the inhabitants, to not want to offer you hospitality."[1]

A meditation which grips our hearts and invites us simply to live by loving others.

1. Mère Bordenave, p. 144.

Chapter VII

To Jesus through Mary

Selected visitors

When she joined Saint-Gildard, where she had come for seclusion, the Superiors had promised Sister Marie-Bernard that she would not be bothered by visitors except in exceptional cases. If she had been preserved from their insensitivity when in the infirmary, she was far more exposed in her role of sacristan. Such as the day when a lady came to Saint-Gildard to meet her. Seeing a group of Sisters in the cloister, she addressed one of them : "Could one of you please tell me which is Sister Marie-Bernard?

"You want to see Sister Marie-Bernard? Ah, very good! Very good!" she answered, evasively. And discretely left the group.

When she didn't come back, the lady asked another Sister the same question. This one replied,

"Sister Marie-Bernard? But you have just spoken to her!... You saw her leave. I wouldn't count on her coming back." It was indeed she who had so deftly escaped, as she always did in these cases[1].

---

1. H. Lasserre, *Bernadette*, p. 276 to 283.

There were also those who hid in a corridor at a moment when she was due to walk by. One day, she noticed a group behind the door of the refectory from whence the Sisters had just started to leave. Her first reaction was to flee to the opposite side, whispering her distaste to her neighbour : "They come to see me like they would look at a strange beast". Then, drawing on her reserves of patience, "Oh, so be it! If I am to be paraded like a beast, at least I am the beast of the good God!" And she walked in front of them, pretending to ignore them.

On certain occasions, when the Mother Superior informed her that a secular person wished to meet her, she sought an appropriate pretext which with to escape. However, when the request came from Bishops, she complied without prevarication. But she didn't hide her displeasure from those who were with her at the time. "These poor Bishops," she would murmur, "they would be better employed staying in their palaces!"[1]

When Sister Marie-Bernard was confined to her bed during her attacks, the Mother Superior refrained from sending her any visitors. She made just one exception, the day a lady came accompanied by her little Madeleine, aged around six or seven, who confessed her bitter disappointment at not having been able to meet her. To console her, the Mother Superior allowed her daughter to visit the patient.

Madeleine asked Sister Marie-Bernard the question right away :

---

1. P. O. Nevers, p. 1037.

"My Sister, have you seen the Holy Virgin?"

"Yes"

"Was she beautiful?"

"So beautiful that, when one has seen her once, one is impatient to die to see her again!"[1]

Once Sister Marie-Bernard had promised her that she would pray for her and her mother, the little girl left the room walking backwards, to be able to contemplate for the longest possible moment, and imprint in her memory, the beautiful face of she who had seen the invisible.

"What I saw was much more lovely"

Sister Marie-Bernard was never far from Lourdes in her heart and in her thoughts. She maintained close contact with her loved ones. She encouraged them to live in harmony, reminded her brothers when they forgot to write to her, offered them advice for their futures. She consoled Joseph and Toinette who lost all of their children, one after another.

Her health had improved by July 1876, she could have travelled to Lourdes with a group of the Sisters of Saint-Gildard who were accompanying their new bishop, for the consecration of the basilica and the crowning of the statue. She refused to participate in the journey. Lourdes no longer belonged to her. She had received the message of Mary. She had transmitted it to mankind. She then retired to Nevers to live the message. Only the Immaculate

---

1. Lasserre, see note 1, p. 65.

Conception should remain illuminated there, to draw the masses to her Son.

She contented herself with giving Father Perreau, who celebrated daily mass at the community, letters for her family, for the Sisters of the Hospice and for Father Peyramale. When he returned, the priest gave her news of all these people, and passed on the hundreds of affectionate messages, including that of Father Peyramale : "Tell her that she is still my child and that I bless her."[1]

A Sister who had been lucky enough to participate in these grandiose celebrations, said to her on her return, "So many beautiful things that took place at the grotto. What a shame that you never saw them!"

"My Sister, don't pity me!" she replied "What I saw was much more lovely."[5]

At the whim of the seasons

Sister Marie-Bernard's health was to know only rare periods of calm. A tumour on the knee, added to her ailments, meaning that she had to walk with a crutch. Sometimes her bouts of asthma followed attacks of haemoptysis, when they didn't occur at the same time. She was then condemned to spending days and nights in bed which, with its white curtains drawn, she called her "white chapel". To strengthen her prayer in such painful moments, she had hung a crucifix, images of Mary, her Patron Saint, and

1. A. Perreau, P. O. Nevers, p. 94.
2. H. Lasserre, p. 305.

some other illustrations of the Passion and the Eucharist. During her hours of rest, she painted or embroidered little fabric hearts, that the Sisters distributed to visitors. During Lent she painted and engraved "Easter eggs" for children in the orphanage.

When the good weather returned, she got out of bed to do a few chores around the house, supporting herself on canes. She walked in the garden, admired the flowers, prayed to Saint Joseph in his oratory, or Mary before the statue of Our Lady of the Water. When she was strong enough, she joined the recreation of the novices, who she entertained with her songs in patois, her funny stories, or her imitations of Doctor Saint-Cyr. When the weather was poor, she took her place in the sewing room to decorate altar cloths, or embroider albs in lace : marvellous items!

It was during one of these periods of calm that she learnt of the death of Father Peyramale. The Sister who came to tell her observed her reaction : "She made just a low cry, a moan of weakness : 'Oh, my Father' I have never heard such a distressing sound. She fell to her knees, holding her hands together, felled by the blow of this death."[1]

It was September 8th 1876, the day when the Church celebrates the birth of Mary.

Like a bird with broken wings

When Sister Marie-Bernard was confined to bed, she won the admiration of the nurse who praised her patience:

---

1. H. Lasserre, p. 322-323.

"How accepting you are:" she said to her one day. In her answer, Sister Marie-Bernard did not hide the limits of her human nature :

"Yes, by force! But try as I might to renew my sacrifice and pretend that I am accepting... I realise that it is not true... especially when I am being tormented like today."

"And who is tormenting you?"

"Don't you see the sunbeam which has just wandered across my bed, mocking me, telling me that it is lovely outside and that I have to stay here in my prison? And these birds singing to call me outside, I who am in a cage, can't you hear them?"[1]

Certainly, the physical inactivity was a burden for Sister Marie-Bernard. But what she deplored even more was the feeling of having no use within the community. After having been the instrument for broadcasting such a beautiful message of hope, she was, in her own words "good for nothing". Like a broom put back behind the door after having been used.

Our first impulse doesn't belong to us

At Lourdes, the Virgin had asked young Bernadette to pray for sinners, and over the years she had developed an ever more pronounced belief that she was terribly sinful. She had great difficulty in restraining her verbal reaction at each annoyance. Observations made by some of her companions illustrate this. One day, a Sister, admitting to

---

1. H. Lasserre, p. 296.

her that she strongly admired her, invited her to touch her rosary, on the pretext of having her see how rusty it was. The reaction was immediate : "Say it more often and it won't rust."[1]

Another time, a Sister who saw her taking snuff (on the orders of doctor Saint-Cyr), said to her, "My Sister, you will not be canonised". The response burst forth, "And you who does not take snuff, you will be canonised, without doubt?"

These moments of ill humour, for which she wou d immediately beg pardon, were for her simply the illust a-tion of our "first impulse [which] doesn't belong to u ."[2]

But there remained the second impulse, which was not always in accordance with the evangelical ideal.

A sinner wants to sin

Sister Marie-Bernard had maintained a certain over-sensitivity combined with an opinionated nature that she described as stubbornness. She was tormented by the feeling that she had been an unworthy messenger of the Immaculate Conception. "I have received so much fortune! I fear that I am unworthy."[3]

This opinion of herself had generated such anguish that it troubled even her sleep and nothing, including prayer, could ease it... Until the day that she heard the

---

1. E. Guynot, *Souvenirs inédits*, p. 28-29.

2. *Bernadette disait*, Couvent de Saint-Gildard, p. 65.

3. P. O. Nevers, p. 288.

sermon of the new Chaplain of the community, Father Fèvre.

On leaving the chapel, she could not hide her joy from the Sister on whose arm she was leaning to walk. "Oh, I am so happy! The Chaplain said that when we do not want to sin, we don't."

"Yes, I heard that. And so?"

"So, I never wanted to commit a sin, therefore I have never committed any."[1]

Such guidance was to be a precious help for her in becoming more receptive to this source of living water that is Christ. After having liberated her conscience of the muddy traces of scruples that obstructed it, he invited her to profess greater trust in his merciful love.

Take steps towards God

Sister Marie-Bernard was, in all serenity, working on freeing herself of these residues of pride which her character provoked. As is proven by the resolutions she noted in a notebook, "The more I lower myself, more I will grow in Jesus' heart." "When faced with scorn or humiliation... thank [him] immediately as if it were grace : bear a prickly comment to make a step towards [him]."[2]

She made steps towards him, by moving further along the path of detachment from oneself. "I will go," she wrote, "before those who have humiliated me, [I will be]

1. P. O. Nevers, p. 208.
2. Mère Bordenave, p. 159.

good for them, not for the people themselves but for love of Our Lord." "[I remind myself] often of these words : Only God is good, and from him I await my reward."[1]

The following incident is indicative of the fruits of Sister Marie-Bernard's efforts to achieve that "holy indifference" as it is called by theologians. One day when she was fit enough, she was climbing the stairs leaning on the arm of a Sister to return to the infirmary. They met the Mother Superior who called them "useless people". Her companion burst into tears. She hurried to console her. "You cry for such a little thing. Oh... you will see many more!"[2]

Sister Marie-Bernard did not miss an occasion to achieve this detachment from oneself, even in terms of taste. One day, a Sister let the porridge that she was preparing for her, burn."I was very upset," admitted the guilty party, "to present her with such an offering, but she took it with a laugh and ate it as if it was delicious."[3]

Another day it was a burnt hot chocolate that she accepted to drink without complaint. "It is better than the other times,"[4] she said with a bitter smile. This remark had a stronger impact on the culprit that the strongest reprimand would have had.

An improvement in her health allowed her, on September 8th, to pronounce her eternal vows in the chapel of the community.

---

1. Mère Bordenave, p. 198.
2. P. A. Nevers, p. 1239.
3. Mère Bordenave, p. 198.
4. Mère Bordenave, p. 166.

The perfumes of friendship

This "holy indifference" did not mean however that Sister Marie-Bernard showed no interest in those special moments that are created by friendship or family affection. Towards All Saints Day in 1878, a Sister, who knew how much she loved flowers, picked her a bouquet of violets which had flowered again in the mild autumn weather. She had a novice take them to the infirmary with this message, "My dear Sister, today it is your saint's day, as it is All Saint's day". The next day, Sister Marie-Bernard had the same novice deliver a note to her saying, "If it is my saint's day, it is also yours. Please accept half of my cake".[1]

Towards the end of the year she had to return to the infirmary. On December 18th she had the pleasant surprise of an unexpected visitor : her brother, Jean-Marie. She was so weak that she had to be taken to the parlour in a chair. We can imagine the joy of seeing each other again, and her brother's worry, seeing her so weakened.

On March 18th 1879, Toinette and Joseph Sabathé, after hearing the pessimistic news from Jean-Marie, came to Nevers themselves. Fearing that they would never see her again, they wanted to embrace her one last time, and sooth their injured hearts : they had just lost their fifth child. She was not able to provide them with the consolation that they craved, she was barely able to communicate with them by gesture and regard. For Toinette, as for

1. *Id, ibid.*

Jean-Marie, it was their last meeting with this elder sister who was so dear to their hearts.

At the heart of Love

Sister Marie-Bernard was entering the last stage of her earthly existence. Her stomach refused all nourishment. Her coughing fits and haemoptysis, combined with frequent asthma attacks weakened her and suffocated her. The stabbing pains in her paralysed knee were so violent when she was lying down that she was moved to a chair for a good part of the day. Her moral suffering was as intense as her physical pain. Like Jesus in the Garden of Gethsemane, she felt abandoned by God. But it was in this union with the Son that she rediscovered the Father: "Jesus, in distress yet at the same time the refuge for souls in distress, your love teaches me that it is in your abandonment that I will find the strength that I need to bear my own..."[1]

It is to the Heart of Jesus that she confided her distress: "Jesus, I am suffering and I love you... it is towards your Heart that my endless groans are directed[2]" She also turned to Mary : "Mother of pain, here is your child who can't go on... May I remain with you at the foot of the cross?"[3]

---

1. E. Guynot, *Souvenirs inédits*, p. 244.
2. P. O. Nevers, p. 1156.
3. *Carnet de notes intimes*, Sœurs de Saint-Gildard, p. 10.

The Eucharist was, for her, a special way of achieving this union with God that she was seeking : it was, according to one of her companions, "the very oxygen of her soul."[1] In her "white chapel" after having received it, she clasped her hands. Indifferent to her surroundings, she seemed to be in conversation with an invisible being. To one Sister, who expressed astonishment at her attitude, she explained, "I believe it is the Holy Virgin who gives me Baby Jesus. I welcome him. I speak to him and he speaks to me... You have to[welcome him]. It is in our interest to give him a warm welcome, because we need him to pay our rent."[2]

Yes, Sister Marie-Bernard was already on her way to the "other world". She was at the foot of the cross with Mary. On March 28th she received the Last Rites for the fifth time, which she accepted only to gain the strength to die well. And not, as on the previous occasions, to restore her health.

From the Monday of Holy Week, April 6th 1879, her symptoms worsened. Her pain was sometimes beyond her tolerance. At these moments she said to the nurse : "Look in your drug cabinet and find something to strengthen me. I can't breathe I feel so weak. Ah! If you could just find something to ease my back! I am in agony."[3]

This search for pain relief makes her seem so much closer to us...and so human! As does her attitude towards

1. Sœur B. Dalias, P. A. Nevers, p. 1468.
2. Sœur V. Garros, P. O. Neves, p. 1229.
3. P. O. Nevers, p. 1051.

the Sister who watched over her at night, without closing her eyes for a second : she asked for one more inclined to sleep to take her place.

To Jesus through Mary

The visits from the chaplain soothed her a little. On Holy Tuesday, he urged her, as tactfully as possible, to sacrifice her life. Her answer inspired as much surprise in him as it did respect : "But, my Father, there is no sacrifice in leaving this life where it is a struggle not to offend God, and where we encounter so many pathways for doing so."[1]

"That is for sure" he replied. "It must not be a sacrifice to go and enjoy for ever the eternal splendours of God... And you, my Sister, without ever having contemplated the face of the Most High, yet you know something of what is divine goodness?"

"Yes," she replied after a moment of silence, "and it is that memory which consoles me and turns my heart towards hope."[2]

Sister Marie-Bernard had indeed contemplated the reflection of divine goodness in the face of Mary which had led her to her Son. From then on, she had only one desire : to unite herself more intensely with him. She ordered all the images and other objects that she had placed in her "white chapel" to support her prayer to be

---

1. H. Lasserre, p. 337.
2. H. Lasserre, p. 337.

removed...with the exception of her crucifix: "Now," she said to those who were with her "I have no need of anything else except that".[1]

On Easter Monday, she admitted to her nurses how extremely weak she felt : "I have been ground like a grain of wheat"[2]: the last allusion to the mill of her childhood. On the Wednesday she was sitting in her armchair, to relieve her bedsores and help her to breathe easier. Towards 1.30pm the chaplain came to sit with her. She was heard to murmur : "My Jesus, oh, how I love him![3]

She took her crucifix in her hands and leant forwards to kiss it, assisted by a Sister who held her arm. Then in a weak and trembling voice, she abandoned herself to Mary : "Mother of God, pray for me, poor sinner... poor sinner..." Two large tears rolled down her cheeks. These were her last words. Her last tears. Her last breath. She was thirty five. It was 3.15 on the afternoon of April 16th 1879.

---

1. P. A. Nevers, p. 847.
2. P. A. Nevers, p. 1106.
3. Mère Bordenave, p. 287.

Content

This work has been typeset
by Atlant'Communication
of Sables-d'Olonne in Vendée, France

Achevé d'imprimer en France
le 18 février 2010
sur les presses de

52200 Langres - Saints-Geosmes
Dépôt légal : septembre 2007 - N° d'imprimeur : 8378